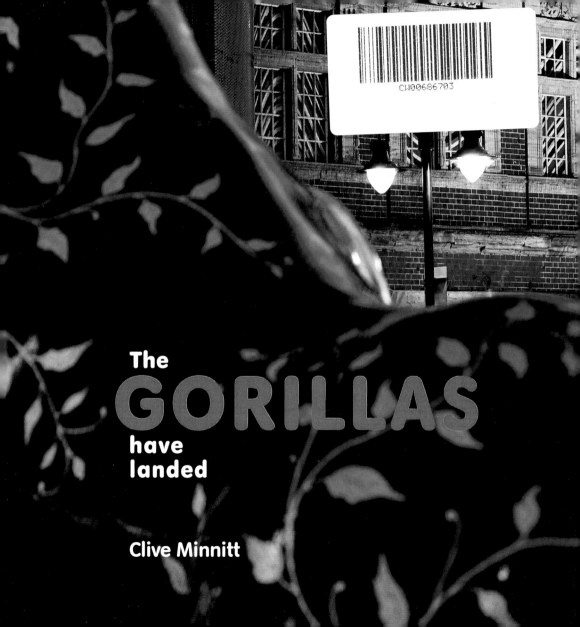

The
GORILLAS
have
landed

Clive Minnitt

Introduction

There have been strange and wondrous goings-on in the city of Bristol during the summer of 2011. We have been exposed to vibrant and exciting collections of art, bringing a riot of colour to the streets and beaming smiles to faces.

Bristol is renowned for being the home of Banksy, now an internationally famous artist, and for the proliferation of street art of the highest quality. The outstanding success of the Banksy exhibition at the City Museum & Art Gallery appears to have sparked a forward-thinking decision by the city's council to actively encourage an outpouring of painterly skills.

Well-known street artists from Bristol and abroad were invited to radically change the look of one of the city's most tired and drab-looking thoroughfares, Nelson Street. The result was an overnight success.

The burgeoning reputation of many talented local artists received a further boost with the exciting arrival of a band of gorillas. I have to admit to resorting to the Internet to discover the collective noun and felt that band was entirely appropriate – a merrier band of creatures one could not imagine!

Bristol Zoo is celebrating its 175th Anniversary and what better way to mark the occasion than to persuade 61 gorillas to leave their own planet behind and meet the people who live in and around Bristol. Invitation accepted, the gorillas requested a change of attire and so a host of artists were invited to design new outfits that would be far more suitable for their new surroundings.

It wasn't long before some of the gorillas decided that city-life wasn't very cool; they upped sticks and headed for pastures new. Sadly there were no new pastures to be found and one of them ended up in Sodding Chip-berry, mistakenly believing there might be food on offer.

Another wasn't able to cope with continually being asked, "Awright?" She sought a doctor and found herself in the village of Pill. One small group were determined to make a break for it and took a bus as far as Birmingham where they were last spotted seen walking around in a state of extreme anxiety after seeing a sign for the bull-ring.

Meeting the gorillas became the 'in' thing to be seen doing in Bristol. No one was anyone until they had introduced themselves to all the gorillas. It has become a city full of 'trainspotters' delighting in the simple yet meaningful tick. Gorillas and ticks don't usually get on.

Having the gorillas spend time in our communities has enabled us to learn more about their culture. But what have they learnt about our own odd ways? The gorillas witnessed cars being triple-parked followed by mobile phone/camera-wielding parents and children jumping out whilst uttering the words "say cheese" as they stood next to, or lay prostrate, under them.

Their eyes popped at the sight of scantily clad athletes racing from one gorilla to the next ticking them off. Gorillas aren't used to being ticked off and can usually do whatever they want! This often happened late in the evening when most people appeared to smile more and walk in a funny way whilst drinking strange brown liquid.

I was asked by one inquisitive gorilla why they each had to stand on a plinth. I explained that although the word 'plinth' must have been very difficult for her to wrap her extremely long tongue around, it was vital that she understood the human dictionary definition: Plinth noun. Son of Queen. E.g. Charlth. So, I told her that they were here by royal request. She liked that.

The following pages give an insight into the lives and personalities of the gorillas during their time in the public eye. Remember, the gorillas have not gone away; they are still in our midst, hiding whilst contemplating their next move. In Bristol, things are not what they used to be – the gorillas have landed!

Customer Information Point

15

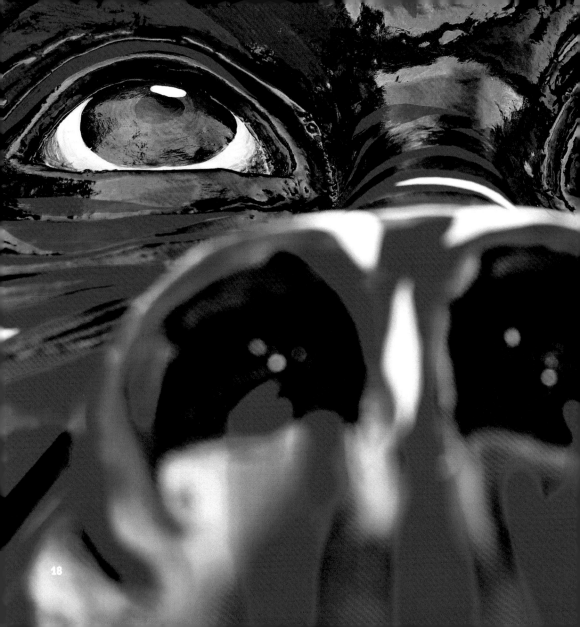

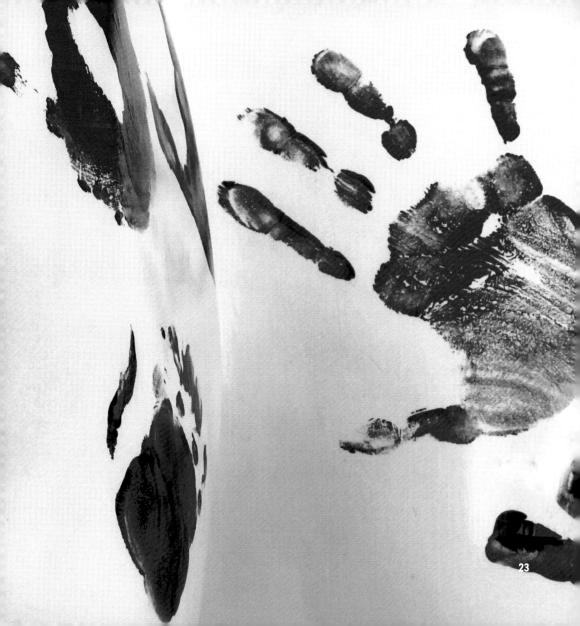

bcfc megastore

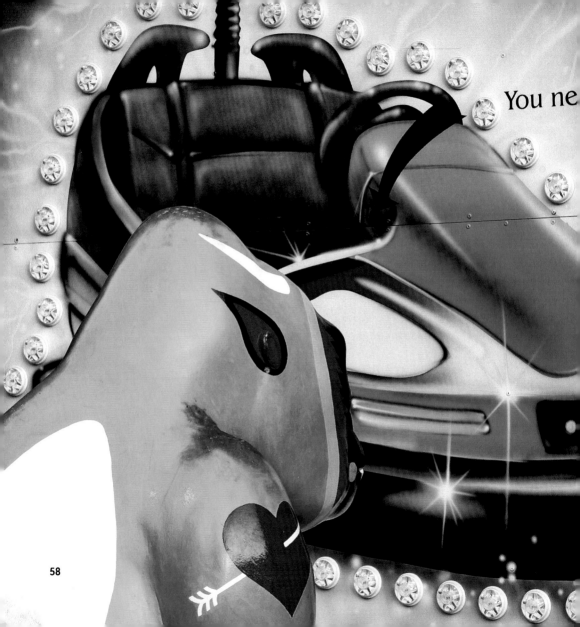

You ne

Bristol &
news &
media

LIM

12

BRIST

... with tradition

63

About Clive Minnitt

Clive Minnitt is a freelance photographer and writer living in Bristol, England. Clive's first book, *Clevedon Pier – A celebration of England's finest pier* (ISBN: 978-0954101138) was published in March 2008, and may be purchased from www.minnitt.co.uk. "What a lovely book – it was an honour to be involved even in such a minor way" – Griff Rhys Jones.

A second book, *Finding the Picture* (ISBN: 978-1902538587) was published in November 2009, and is aimed at every photographer who needs a helping hand in identifying suitable subject matter to photograph. The book is jointly written and photographed by Clive and his good friend and fellow Light & Land tour leader, Phil Malpas. It is lavishly illustrated with fine-art colour photography. More recently (May 2010) Clive has contributed images and text to *Travel Photography Masterclass* (ISBN: 978-1902538594). Both books are available from www.amazon.com.

His most recent book, *Isle of Sark*, was also published jointly with Phil Malpas following a visit to the Channel Islands in 2011. The book is available from either www.minnitt.co.uk or www.blurb.com

In May 2002, Clive led his first photographic holiday for the UK based company Light & Land for whom he has become one of the most established tour leaders. Clive has led over 40 tours and workshops to many locations across the UK, Europe, USA and Cuba. If you would like to join Clive on a photographic experience of a lifetime please visit www.lightandland.co.uk to see which tours are presently on offer.

Many magazines have featured Clive's work and he currently has a regular On Location column in *Outdoor Photography* magazine. He also presents his images and photographic techniques to many organisations and societies, including the National Trust.

To see more of Clive's work or purchase a copy of this book please visit
www.minnitt.co.uk

Photographic notes

For those of you who might be interested, here are some additional notes about the photographs in this book…

This project was a great example of having to work within a short timeframe. All images were taken between 12.08.11 to 06.09.11. Most of the images for this book were taken after planning my visits to each location. Time of day, weather conditions, sunrise and sunset times, tides (e.g. Pill) and opening hours of public buildings were all given careful consideration. Very few were as a result of simply turning up and hoping for the best.

My challenge was to make a series of interesting photographs of the gorillas without including the supporting plinths.

All images were captured using a Panasonic Lumix GF1 body with a series of interchangeable lenses from wide angle to telephoto. When contrast management was needed to ensure a usable exposure I used the Lee ND (Neutral Density) graduated filters. I often used a polarising filter to help reduce the large amount of glare (bright light) reflecting from the gorillas, even in dull conditions.

The digital files were pre-processed in Panasonic's SILKYPIX Developer software (to convert the RAW files). Minimal post-processing work was carried out in Adobe Photoshop before converting the files to a format suitable for printing in this book.

Acknowledgements

I would like to thank:-

Eddie Ephraums – for his excellent design.

Phil Malpas, for invaluable website and admin help.

Andy Brindle and all the crew at Clifton Colour for the support I've received during this project. I'm going to return it to them shortly.

Martin Bates, for his proofreading skills.

The creators of this magical outdoor art event; Bristol Zoo, Wild in Art, Bristol City Council, sponsors, local businesses and schools, and any others I may have inadvertently omitted.

Chris Wilkinson, the sculptor, and all the local artists who brought the gorillas to life.

All those people I met whilst photographing the gorillas. They were a never-ending source of enthusiasm, energy and good-natured aping around. I hope they all achieved their goals.

Each of you who has purchased this book – you are adding to the donations to two deserving charities. I hope you have enjoyed the odd titter or two.

Donation to charities

10% of profits will be donated to two
designated charities, equally split between
Bristol Zoo gorilla conservation projects and
Wallace & Gromit's Grand Appeal (Bristol Royal
Hospital for Children & Neonatal Intensive Care
Unit (NICU) at St. Michael's Hospital).

First published in Great Britain 2011
by Clive Minnitt Books
15 Longfield Road, Bishopston, Bristol BS7 9AG

ISBN 978-0-9570620-0-9

Design and production by Eddie Ephraums,
Envisage Books

Printed by Advantage Digital Print